ISBN 978-1-331-85616-0
PIBN 10242752

1 MONTH OF
FREE
READING

at

www.ForgottenBooks.com

By purchasing this book you are eligible for one month membership to ForgottenBooks.com, giving you unlimited access to our entire collection of over 700,000 titles via our web site and mobile apps.

To claim your free month visit:

www.forgottenbooks.com/free242752

Similar Books Are Available from
www.forgottenbooks.com

Pioneer Colored Christians

BY

HARRIET PARKS MILLER

"The primitive order with its picturesque
types, has passed with the days that are
dust. The mirthful banjo is mute, and the
laughter, songs, and shouts of the old plantation quarters no longer float out on the
evening air."

CLARKSVILLE, TENN.
W. P. TITUS, PRINTER AND BINDER
—1911—

TO THE READER.

In the busy rush of life, the virtues of single individuals too often escape notice, or make but slight impression on the minds of their contemporaries. It is in after years, when the actors are dead and gone, that their virtues shine forth, and speak from the silence, through the pen of some one who catches them before it is too late.

No history is richer, or more beautiful, than that written of lives led by wisdom, and goodness.

The writing of this little book is inspired by a desire to perpetuate, as examples, the lives of such people. While the trend of my thoughts will center around one special family, —the Carrs—I shall not omit honorable mention of other colored citizens, who walked upright among their fellow men.

I shall also make mention of leading white people who befriended the colored race in its early struggles for religious liberty.

I write with the hope, that what I say, will have a tendency to deepen the sympathy, and kind feeling which should ever exist between the two races living together in the South.

THE AUTHOR.

Port Royal, Tenn., July, 1911.

CONTENTS

CHAPTER I.

CHAPTER II.

3

Shoe Bend" of Red River, by permission of Mr. William Weatherford, its owner. Mode of making a living. Joins Red River Church, and is ordained to preach. Invitation by Mr. E. L. Fort, to preach on his premises.

Chapter III.

Worship of the two races together, in ante-bellum times.

Department in white churches for colored worshippers.

Civil war brings changes, and they have churches and schools of their own.

Sketch of Dr. P. F. Norfleet, of Port Royal, Tenn., who gave land on which to build Mount Zion, one of the first colored churches in Middle Tennessee.

Amusing story of Mr. and Mrs. Ed. Hawkins, of Turnersville, Robertson county, Tenn.

Chapter IV.

Aunt Kitty describes her vision, or dream, in which the future Mount Zion appeared to her. It takes tangible form, and Rev. Horace Carr assembles his people under a large white oak tree on the lot donated by Dr. Norfleet, and assisted by Revs. Chess Ware, and Ben Thomas, of Guthrie, Ky., organizes the church.

First house of worship soon erected. Too small, and later torn away to give place to larger building.

Two buildings burned, but the faithful Christians did not lose hope.

List of charter members.

Younger generation following the religious footsteps of their ancestors.

Mr. William Bourne gives lot for burying ground.

CHAPTER V.

Rev. Althens Carr.

Birth and early life. Obtains education under great difficulties.

An eloquent pulpit orator.

Two funeral sermons heard by the writer.

William, and Jack Northington, two worthy brothers.

Why Uncle Arter Northington was called "Paul."

CHAPTER VI.

Rev. Horace Carr tells of an antebellum corn shucking on Mr. Waters' farm.

Describes great excitement in Port Royal neighborhood, the night the stars fell, November, 1833.

CHAPTERS III.

Rev. J. W. Carr.

CHAPTER I.

―――――

―――――

The people whom you will meet in this little book did not live in fancy.

They were humble instruments through whom God sent a message clear, and strong, that will go on, and on, through the coming years.

Realizing the rapidity with which the good old colored types were passing away, I went one September afternoon, 1901, to see Aunt Kitty Carr, for the purpose of obtaining some interesting facts concerning herself, and her remarkable family.

Her husband, Uncle Horace Carr, had been dead twenty-four years, and she was then living with her son Horace, at his farm on Red River, a mile or two from Port Royal, Tennessee.

I found her on the back porch peeling peaches to dry, and when I made known to her the intent of my visit, she was amused, and said, "Lor Miss

8

Aunt Kitty Carr.

Harriet, what am *I* say, that will be worth reading in a book?"

On assuring her of the esteem in which she and her family were held, and the importance of such lives being left on tangible record, she seemed willing to tell me, in her quaint way, what I wished to know.

Aunt Kitty was a small yellow woman, of refined features, and dignified bearing.

She spoke as follows:

"Of course you have heard that I was free born?"

"Yes," I replied, "you were the first free born person of your race, that I ever saw."

"I was born near Spottssylvania, Virginia, in 1815. That's been a *long* time ago. I'll soon be eighty-six years old. My children, and grandchildren are kind to me, and don't want me to work, but I am not satisfied to sit idle.

My father was a Frenchman of some importance, by the name of Truell; my only recollection of him was his long curly hair that came down to his shoulders. My mother was free born, and gave me away.

"One bright spring day she was sweeping her front yard, and I, a little girl of six years, was taking up the trash, that she swept together, when a pretty white girl sixteen, or seventeen, rode past the gate, and called for a drink of water. As she handed the drinking gourd back, she said, 'That's a handy little girl you have there, I wish you'd give her to me.' 'All right,' mother replied, and the lady passed on, and nothing more was thought of it, till nearly a year afterward, a nice covered wagon drove up to our gate, and the same lady called for me

"A few days before, she had married a Mr. Edmond Winston, and they were going to house-keeping.

"My mother gathered together my little budget. of clother, and handed little Kitty, and the clothes over to the colored driver, saying, 'Here take her.'

"And they took me; I have never thought mother acted right.

"The new married couple lived in Virginia about a year after that, when they decided to come to Tennessee, and brought me with them. We came a long journey, in that same covered wagon, and settled in District No. 1, Montgomery county, near where Fortson's Spring now is.

"They were as kind to me, as they could be, and I was content to stay with them.

"After coming to Tennessee, Mr. Winston did not live very long, and his widow, after a respectable time, married a Mr. Coleman, grandfather of the first Mrs. Polk Prince, and great grandfather of Mrs. Lewis Downer, of Guthrie, Ky.

"But I was always called Kitty Winston. The Colemans and Johnsons were related, and through their visiting from Fortson Spring neighborhood to Spring Creek, farther down toward Clarksville, I met my lifetime companion.

"He was the property of Mr. Aquilla Johnson, of Spring Creek, and was first known as Horace Johnson.

"We were married when we were both quite young. Soon after our marriage, it was necessary to make a division of the property, and Mr. Johnson sold my husband to Mr. James Carr, of Port Royal, grandfather of Mr. Ed, and Ross Bourne.

We had not been long settled down to quiet, peaceable living in our little cabin home, when it began to be whispered around among a cruel class of white people called overseers, that I could be deprived of my free birth right, and made a slave. Of course it made me very unhappy, and I prayed earnestly over the matter.

I went to sertain good white friends who had known me longest, and laid the case before them, and they advised me to go to Esq. Dick Blount, of Fortson's Spring, and he would fix up some papers that would establish my freedom for all time to come.

"I put out for the Blount home in haste, my husband going with me. When we reached there, a member of the Esquire's family told me he was drunk, but if I could wait an hour or two, he might be sober enough to talk to me. Of course I waited. We were seated in the back yard, and a quiet couple we were, for it was a solemn time in our lives.

"By, and by, we saw the Esquire came out on the back porch, and washed his face. I whispered and asked Horace, if he reckoned he was washing the drunk off.

"We walked up to the door, and told our mission; Esq. Blount advised us to go on to Clarks ville, and said he would follow on shortly.

"We waited, and waited, on the Court House steps, and I had about decided he was not coming, when we looked up the street, and saw him.

"He took an iron square, and measured my height, wrote a description of my features, and asked me if there were any scars on my body. I knew of none, except a small one the size of a silver dime, on the back of my neck, caused from the deep burning of a fly blister. I showed him that.

"He kindly fixed up the papers, and handed

them to me. I kept them closely guarded, till my oldest daughter, Mary Waters, was going to move to the State of Ohio to live, and not knowing what might happen to her there, she asked me for them, and I willingly gave them to her. I always regretted that I did not keep a copy, for it would be a curiosity to the present generation."

As she quietly sat, and told me all this, her grand daughter, Eleanora Carr Johnson, was an attentive listener, never having before, heard such details of antebellum history. The afternoon seemed too short; so pleasant was the interview that I regretted not having gone oftener, to see her. She referred incidentally to a little prayer book, "Morning and Night Watches," by Rev. J. R. McDuff, D. D., from which I had often read to her, in days gone by, and expressed a desire to hear a certain chapter once more.

Feeling that she would enjoy hearing it, I had carried the little book along with me, and read to her as follows: "May it be mine to cheerfully follow the footsteps of the guiding Shepherd through the darkest, loneliest road, and amidst thickest sorrows may I have grace to say, 'Though He slay me, yet will I trust in Him.'"

"Lord, increase my faith, let it rise above all trials, and difficulties. And if they arise, may they only drive me closer to Him who has promised to make me more than conqueror. I am a pilgrim, pitching my tent day, by day, nearer heaven, imbibing every day more of the pilgrim character, and longing more for the pilgrim's rest.

"May I be enabled to say, with the chastened spirit of a passing world, 'Here I have no continuing city.'

"May this assurance reconcile me to all things.

"Lord, hasten Thy coming, and Thy kingdom.

"Scatter the darkness that is hovering over heathen nations.

"Stand by Thy Missionary servants. Enable us all, to be living more from day to day, on Thy grace, to rely on Thy guiding arm with more childlike confidence, looking with a more simple faith to Thy finished work.

"Be the God of all near, and dear to me.

"May all my ties of blood, scattered far and wide over the earth, be able to claim a spiritual relationship with Thee, so that those earthly bonds of attachment, which sooner or later, must snap asunder here, be renewed, and perpetuated before the great white throne."

As I read, she clasped her hands and looked reverently upward, as if her soul were drinking in the spirit of the great writer.

She followed me to the front gate, and thanked me for my visit.

It was the last time I ever saw her.

CHAPTER II.

"MARK THE PERFECT MAN, AND BEHOLD THE UPRIGHT, FOR THE END OF THAT MAN IS PEACE."

Having given my opening chapter to an interview with Aunt Kitty, I will now tell of her husband, Rev. Horace Carr, who was born on the Aquilla Johnson farm, on Spring Creek, in District No. 1, Montgomery county, Tenn., 1812. By way of explanation, I will state that white children, in antebellum times, were taught by their parents, to call middle aged colored people Aunt, and Uncle; hence "Aunt Kitty," and "Uncle Horace," by the writer.

From early childhood, Uncle Horace was noted for his truth, and honesty.

In maturer years, strongers who met him on the highway, were impressed by his polite manners, and upright countenance.

The late Col. Jno. F. House, of Clarksville, once said of him, that he had the dignified bearing of African royalty.

He was married during the early 30's, and was often heard to say, that God never sent him a greater blessing than Kitty Winston.

It will be remembered that the offspring of a free born parent, either mother, or father, was also free, and after several sons, and daughters were given to Aunt Kitty, and Uncle Horace, they desired to be in a home of their own; Mrs. Carr having become a widow, she was administratrix of a very nice little estate, and Uncle Horace was one of her most valuable slaves, and when it was talked around that he wished to hire himself from his mistress, very few believed that she would consent for him to leave the premises.

He first talked to influential citizens of his neighborhood, as to the possibility of securing a suitable location for his humble home, and Dr. P. F. Norfleet, of Port Royal, promised to use his influence in that direction.

So he sent to Mr. William Weatherford, owner of a fine farm on Red River, in sight of Port Royal, and laid the case before him.

In the meantime, Uncle Horace summoned up courage enough to propose hiring himself from Miss Nancy, as he called Mrs. Carr, for the sum of $200.00, to which she consented.

Mr. Weatherford kindly granted the homestead

Cabin (Aunt Judy's House) on the old Fort Plantation,
in which Rev. Horace Carr preached
his first sermon.

site, near a secluded place on his plantation, known as "Horse Shoe Bend."

A small log house was soon erected, and the Carr family, with their scant belongings went to dwell therein.

And now the problem of making a living confronted them.

How was it to be done?

"We will work, and save, and trust in the Lord," Uncle Horace would say.

And they did.

He made boards, bottomed chairs, did crude carpentering, and kept the ferry on Red River, at Port Royal, during the high water season, while his industrious little wife spun, wove, sold ginger sakes to the village groceries; now, and then, accompanying the stork on its grand mission of leaving rosebud baby girls, and boys in the homes of families, where she remained a week or two, with their mothers, in the capacity of a tender and experienced nurse.

There are many mature men and women in our midst today, who first opened their baby eyes under Aunt Kitty's watch-care.

She and Uncle Horace were economical, and usually saved fifty, or seventy-five dollars, above his promised wages to Mrs. Carr.

On Christmas eve morning, of each year, after

moving to their home near Horse Shoe Bend, he would wend his way quietly back to the old Carr homestead, with his well earned $200.00 for Miss Nancy, who always felt safe in making her Christmas purchases a week or two ahead of the holiday season, knowing he would be true to his promise. And she always had a present for his family, often a pig, with some corn to feed it.

People of that date, were practical, in their present making, at Christmas time. Uncle Horace professed religion when quite young, during a revivial at Red River Church, under the ministry of Elder Réuben Ross, a distinguished pioneer Bapitst who came from North Carolina, to Tennessee, over a century ago.

After his profession, he felt a great desire to preach, and as the years passed, the desire grew stronger, till he felt convinced that he was Divinely called. So about ten years before the Civil War, he was ordained to preach.

His ordination took place in Red River Church, the primitive building on the hillside, a mile or two north west of Adams, Revs. F. C. Plaster, and W. G. Adams, officiating.

There was a large congregation present, and the ceremony was said to have been a very impressive one.

Mr. Lawson Fort was present and took great

interest in the proceedings, and followed Uncle Horace out on the church grounds and said to him:

"Horace, I am a Baptist preacher's son, but I do not belong to any church, though I have great respect for religious people.

"I want to say to you, whenever you feel like preaching, or holding a prayer meeting, come to my house, and feel welcome, and I will see to it that you are not disturbed by patrolers.

"You will understand, Horace, that my negroes are first-class, and I don't care to have a mixed crowd on my premises at night. I guess your little family, and my thirty or forty, will give you a pretty fair congregation. It will be best to hold your meetings in Judy's house, as she has no small children.

"She has her Indigo dye-pots setting around in every corner, but I guess she can move them out.

"Judy prays, Margaret shouts, and John exhorts, so it seems, that among them all, you might get up some pretty good meetings."

"May the Lord abundantly bless you, Mars Lawson, for such kindness to a race striving under difficulties, to serve God," Uncle Horace replied.

Prior to this, he had only held religious services in his own home, but the invitation from Mr.

Fort gave him fresh courage, and he retired that night with thankfulness in his heart, and a firm resolve to live up to the Divine light that had been given him.

Of the two ministers who assisted in Uncle Horace's ordination, I will speak briefly.

Rev. W. S. Adams was the eldest son of Reuben Adams; the latter came to Tennessee from North Carolina in 1812, and settled on the bank of Red River in Robertson county, near where the first old Red River Church building stood.

He was a penniless orphan boy, but by industry, and economy, was soon able to buy a small farm. Land at that date, was very cheap.

He was married early in life, to Miss Priscilla Robinson, who made him a pleasant companion.

In the early 50's, the Edgefield and Kentucky Railroad Co. had civil engineers to blaze the path for the first railroad that ran through this section.

A depot was built, and the little station called Adams, in honor of Mr. Reuben Adams. On account of this railroad passing through his premises, the value of his land was greatly increased, and from that time on, he was able to assist his children financially.

Growing up while his father was poor, Rev. William Adams had but few educational advantages. He professed religion in his youth, and was often heard to remark, that most he knew of the Bible, was learned in Sunday school.

He was twice married, the first time to Miss Batts, of Robertson county, and second, to Miss Kosure, of Madisonville, Ky. Eight or nine children by his first marriage are all dead, while two by his second, also an aged wife, survive him, and live in Texas.

Rev. Adams spent thirty odd years in the ministry. In the early 80's he moved from Robertson county to Nashville.

One morning he rose early, and remarked to his wife, that he felt unusually well, and wished to put in a good day's work among the afflicted of the neighborhood, and spoke of first visiting Mrs. Jones across the street from his home (nee Miss Lizzie Frey), who had been one of his favorite members of Little Hope Church, in Montgomery county.

Soon after breakfast, he stood before a mirror in the family room shaving, when his wife sitting near, noticed him turn suddenly pale, and stagger She assisted him to a chair, and he died almost instantly, from heart failure.

Rev. F. C. Plaster, was born in Logan county, Ky., 1805. He was of humble parentage, and like Rev. Adams, had no educational advantages.

At sixteen years of age, he joined Red River

Church, and at twenty, he felt the Divine call to preach, and so zealous was he, that it was said of him, that while plaining lumber at the carpenter's bench, he kept his open Bible before him, studying the Scriptures while he worked.

He was a man of commanding appearance, and a fine pulpit orator. He was twice married, and was the father of several sons, and daughters, by his first marriage. Both of his wives were Kentuckians, and most estimable women. In 1879, he moved with his family to Fort Deposit, Ala., and from there, a few years later, he passed from earth.

CHAPTER III.

"IN TRAVELING FROM THIS WORLD TO THE NEXT, THE ROAD IS NO WIDER FOR THE PRINCE, THAN THE PEASANT."—*San no Panza.*

In that period of our country's history known as "slave time," the white people encouraged the colored race to serve God, and received its converts into their own churches, and worshipped with them.

In most of the meeting houses, there were galleries, or separate apartments, in which the colored members sat, and listened to the Gospel preached by white ministers.

Their membership was received into the Baptist Associations, on equal terms, and the colored ministers often preached during the several days sessions of these assemblies. Elder Horace Carr did, when the Association was held at Red River Church.

Speaking of the separate apartments in the churches, the writer has a vivid recollection of the orderly colored congregation that occupied the upper gallery of old Harmony Church, three miles south of Port Royal, in Robertson county.

Near the front, could be seen such devout Christians as old Uncle Allen Northington, Aunt Sydney Norfleet, Aunt Sylvia Carney, Aunt Lucy Parks, Aunt Becky Northington, Aunt Cely Northington, etc. It was a rare occurrence that a colored child was seen at church, but you would notice numerous white children sitting in the laps of their good old "Black Mammys" as they called them. But while this Christian brotherhood was being enjoyed, another day was dawning, in which a new order of things was to take place. The primitive order, with its picturesque types, was doomed to pass away. The broad plantation of the old Southern planter was to undergo material changes, and every influence for good was becoming more and more in unison with the great master chord of Christianity.

Surely the hand of Divinity was in it all, or it would not have been so.

The Civil War came on, and the Institution of Slavery was abolished.

It was not only Aunt Kitty Carr, Uncle Granville Wimberly, and a few others, that were referred to, as "free born," but *all* were free!

The desire for schools and churches of their

"Riverside;" home of the late E. L. Fort.

own was awakened, and the right kind of white people were ready, and willing, to lend them a helping hand. Among the first to lead substan tially in this direction, in Montgomery county, was Dr. P. F. Norfleet, of Port Royal.

Brief sketch of this fine old gentleman: Dr. Philip Ford Norfleet was born in the early part of the past century, at his father's homestead on the Nashville road, one and a half miles south of Port Royal. In later years the place was known as the Dr. J. T. Darden farm.

In his early twenties he was sent to a medical college, and was later on considered one of the best physicians of his day

He was a charter member of Harmony Missionary Baptist Church, organized in 1835, and while it was said of him, that he sowed his share of wild oats in early life, after joining the church he doubled his diligence in good works.

He was married during his twenties, to Miss Elvira Hopson, and several children blessed their union.

He was a man of wealth, owning a large cotton plantation near Friar's Point, Mississippi, to which he made annual trips on horseback, usually at crop selling time, and returning with vast sums of money.

Not caring to risk the health of his large and

happy family, in the malarial districts of the Mississippi swamps, he made his home at Port Royal.

The original Norfleet residence, with few exceptions, remains intact, and is at present owned and occupied by Mr. W. E. Alley, a prosperous farmer, and substantial citizen of Montgomery county.

For the benefit of his family, Dr. Norfleet kept a number of efficient servants.

Among them two very refined house maids, Kitty Hopson and Adeline Norfleet; Frank, the carriage driver; Mary, the cook, and Louis, a roustabout.

Of these, only one survive, Adeline, who in her old age, finds no greater pleasure than in talking of her white people.

Although the Norfleets were the acknowledged aristocrats of the country, they were also benevolent to a marked degree.

Apropos of their liberality, I deem it not amiss to mention the case of Ed and Fronie Hawkins, a very unique, feeble minded couple of white people, who lived in a small one-room log cabin, near Turnersville, in Robertson county, and sub sisted mainly on charity.

Mr. Hawkins, familiarly known as "Old Ed," was a tall, lank figure, with a shock of long sandy hair, that hung in strings around his neck, while his sallow complexion and deep set small blue eyes, completed the make-up of an unattractive personality.

Fronie, his dumpy dame, in point of height, measured very little above her husband's slender waist. She had small brown eyes, fair complexion, and an abundant suit of coarse red hair, which she wore in a massive club, or coil, at the nape of her neck, held in place by a rusty horn tuck comb.

About three times a year, they made begging trips to Port Royal, Dr. Norfleet's home being their objective point.

Fronie would generally start a few days in advance of her husband, in order to get her charity donations together.

He would follow later, and help carry them home.

Dr. Norfleet wore white linen suits in summer, and on one occasion, gave Fronie a second hand suit for Ed.

Dr. Norfleet was tall, and his pants legs were long, so she conceived the idea of packing her donations in the legs of those he had given her. She sewed up the legs at the bottom, put a stout loop on the back of the binding at the top, and hung her improvised receptacle on a hook behind the office door; everything that was given to her, she dropped it down the pants legs—sugar, coffee, second-hand clothes, chunks of meet, etc., all in a jumble.

When they were well nigh full, she began to wish for Mr. Hawkins. He came at last, and she led him to look behind the door.

He was delighted, and scarcely taking time to rest from his journey of six miles on a warm day, he placed the well stuffed pants astride his neck, and struck out up the Nashville road, without even bidding Dr. Norfleet's family good bye.

Fronie followed close at his heels, holding by the legs, in her right hand, a fine fat pair of Muscovy ducks, Mrs. Norfleet had given her. On passing Mr. William Brown's residence, just up the road, Mr. Brown's son, Robert, happened to be at the front gate; young Robert Bourne had a keen sense of humor, and their ludicious appearance threw him into such a fit of laughter that he rolled over and over on the ground.

But the Hawkins's kept straight ahead, bound for Turnersville before sunset, but they were doomed to an unexpected delay.

The ducks grew heavy, and Fronie set them down by the roadside to rest her tired arm.

It happened that she stopped at the head of the ten-foot deep gully, just beyond the old Mallory homestead, where the old Harmony

Church road branched off to the right from the main Nashville route   The ducks set to fluttering, and tumbled down the embankment and into the gully, breaking the string that held them together. Ed flew into a rage, because she let them get away, and swore he'd whip her on the spot, if she did' not catch them. She chased them up and down the gully till she was almost exhausted, when a passing fishing party came to her assistance.

The late George Washington's family contributed liberally to the support of this couple, and in speaking of the Washington home, Fronie always referred to it as "the fat house," meaning rich people.

The young people of Port Royal neighborhood, spent many pleasant times in years gone by, masquerading in comic costumes, as Ed and Fronie Hawkins.

They were known far and wide, as a very amusing couple, but when old age came to them, and the liberal friends who had kept "the wolf from their cabin door" had passed away, it became necessary for them to be carried to the county poor house, and from there, I'm sure, their innocent souls went straight to heaven.

CHAPTER IV.

"WHO OF US CAN SAY, WHICH IS PAIRER, THE VISIONS OF HOPE, OR MEMORY? THE ONE MAKES ALL THINGS POSSIBLE, THE OTHER MAKES ALL THINGS REAL."

In the holy hush of that September afternoon, Aunt Kitty told me of a vision that she had, during the middle 60's.

It was my last talk with her, and she seemed so impressed with the memory of it, that she laid aside her peach peeling, and gave her mind, and soul, to the subject so dear to her heart.

She said: "Some people call them dreams, but I call them visions. Ever since God spoke peace to my soul, I had prayed for religious liberty for my people; so great was my desire in this particular direction, that it seemed as a heavy weight that was bowing me down.

"But one night, about midnight, the burden seemed to be lifted from me. The deep darkness drifted away, and it seemed that the sun shone everywhere, and in a certain direction, I saw a long grassy slope stretch far away before me.

"I could not tell at first, what it meant, for I saw nothing but space. By and by, a small tab,e appeared, and seemed to come nearer and nearer.

"I looked away, and wondered, and then I looked again, and a *Bib't* was on the table.

"The third time I cast my eyes, lo and behold! there stood my old man behind the table, the Bible was open, and he was slowly reading from its sacred pages!

"Miss Harriet, this may all sound very strange to you, but that vision was as plain to me, as the sight of you, sitting here before me.

"The old man had been working away from home all the week, so I got up next morning and went about my daily duties without telling my children what I had seen.

"Saturday night he came home, and after holding family prayers, and everything was quiet about the house, I told him of my vision—and listen, oh, it was joy to my soul! He told me that Dr. Norfleet wanted us to have a place of worship, and that he was willing to give us land on which to build a church, about an acre, on the hillside, between Mr. Bourne's spring and Sulphur Fork Creek. And he said that many

31

other white friends would give lumber, and small sums of money.

"Miss Harriet, we re oiced together that Satur day night, as we never had before. We had been reaching our feeble arms toward Heaven a long time, pleading for the blessing that was now in sight."

Thirty odd years had passed, and a new generation had come, but the flight of time only served to sweeten the sound of her story. As I bade her good bye, I was deeply conscious that I would never see her again, for she was growing too feeble to leave home, and I drove off, feeling spiritually benefitted from contact with such a Christian character as Aunt Kitty Carr.

＊　　＊　　＊　　＊　　＊　　＊　　＊

One Autumn afternoon in 1867, a large crowd of the best colored people of Port Royal and surrounding neighborhoods, assembled on the hillside where Mount Zion now stands, and organized the church.

Elder Horace Carr was assisted in the organization by Revs. Chess Ware and Ben Thomas, of Guthrie Ky. Elder Carr stood under a large white oak tree, and led in the movement, while his hearers sat around on rails, logs, stumps, etc.

It was a movement destined to mean much to the colored people of Robertson and Montgomery

Mount Zion, Colored Baptist Church, near
Port Royal, Tennessee.

counties. Located as it was, near the county line, its membership was composed largely of both counties, but since then, other churches have sprung up, and many of the Mount Zion members joined those nearer their homes.

Alfred Pitt (col.) took the contract for building the first house of worship. It was 30x30 feet, and erected in a very short time.

Most of the white citizens of the neighborhood contributed either lumber or small amounts of money, and when the crude little building appeared on the hillside, all eyes turned to Uncle Horace, as the good shepherd to lead the little flock of seventy odd members.

This first church building, was also used for a school-room, in which was taught one of the first colored schools in Middle Tennessee, during what was termed the "Reconstruction Period;" in other words, the years immediately following the Civil War, when both races were adjusting themselves to the changed conditions brought about by the emancipation of the slaves.

This school was taught by Miss Denie Sims, a nice, refined young woman from Clarksville, Tenn., who conducted not only herself, but her school, so well, that she was highly esteemed by both white and colored people of Port Roval neighborhood.

The first building being too small to accommodate the congregations that rapidly increased in numbers, it was torn away' after standing two or three years, and replaced bv one of 36x40 feet.

This stood five years, and was burned at night by unknown parties. Circumstantial evidence pointed strongly to certain people, but there was no positive proof.

After the excitement, incident to such an occurrence, had subsided, Uncle Horace gathered together a portion of his little flock, and cautioned them to say no harsh words, that all would be well, for he felt that the good people who had assisted them before, would do so again, and they would rebuild. They rebuilt on the same foundation, and all went right for a few vears, or, until a band of colored gamblers became a menace to law, and order. So bold did they grow in their wickedness, that one night they actually gambled in front of the church door, from the same light that guided the good minister in reading the Gospel from the sacred desk!

It was more than the Christian congregation could stand, and strenuous measures were taken against the offenders.

That same week Mount Zion again went up in flames, but faith, and persistency, are Life's architects, and the fourth building was erected, and there it stands today, a monument to the courage of a faithful few.

For the benefit of those who would like to know the charter members of Mount Zion Church, I give below a list of their names; true it is, a few may have been overlooked, but in the main, they are as follows

Svdney Allen.

Rev. Horace Carr.

Kitty Carr.

Horace Carr, Jr.

Rev. Althens Carr.

Lucinda Carney.

Sylvia Carnev.

Easter Carney.

Isaac Carnev.

Aleck Carnev.

Ann Dunn.

Judy Fort.

Margaret Fort.

Charlotte Fort.

Katie Fort.

George Francis Fort.

Jim Fort.

Peggy Fort.

Rev. John Fort.

Daniel Fort.

Sampson Fort.

Henry Fort.

Frank Fort.

Sarah Grant.

John Grant.

Bear John Grant.

Nelson Grant.

Vinie Grant.

Wallace Gaines.

Maria Gaines.

Phil Gaines.

Dennis Gaines.

Martha Gaines.

Clarissa Gaines.

Malachi Gaines.

Eliza Gaines.

Eliza Holmes.

Waddy Herring.

Sallie Ann.Herring.

Rachel Izor.

Sam Izor.

Mark Mitchell.

Patsy McGowan.
John McGowan.
Martha Newton.
Sookey Northington.
Vinie Northington.
Caroline Northington.
William Northington.
Jack Northington.
Angeline Northington.
Seely Northington.
Chaney Northington.
Elijah Northington.
Louisanna Northington.
Bettie Northington.

Dennis Northington.
Rebekah Northington.
Allen Northington.
Neptune Northington.
George Northington.
Sam Northington
Almira Northington.
Betsy Neblett.
Kitty Norfleet.
Adeline Norfleet.
Rildy Polk.
Lucy Parks.
Demps Wimberly.
Delphi Waters.

With few exceptions, nearly all of the above charter members had been members of Red River and Harmony churches before the Civil War Scarcely a dozen of them remain with us in the flesh.

During its forty-four years' existence, Mount Zion has had the following pastors:

Rev. Horace Carr.
Rev. Altheus Carr.
Rev. Edmond Northington.
Rev. Paul Dennis.
Rev. George Mimms.
Rev. Turner Parish.
Rev. M. Fox.

Rev. L. Jones.

Rev. A. J. Moore, D. D.

Of the original Deacons, only one is alive, Aleck Carney, the other six in active service are:

Dan Fort.

George Fort.

Demps Fort.

Albert Steward.

Wright Watkins.

Will Randolph.

It is a noticeable fact, that the second and third generations of some of Mount Zion's charter members, are at present among its best workers; as for example, Rev. John Fort's son Dan, and grandson George, upon whose shoulders a father's religious mantle has fallen.

Soon after the donation of land by Dr. Norfleet for Mount Zion Church; Mr. William Bourne, on an adjoining farm, gave land for a colored cemetery.

Mr. Bourne was a citizen of fine standing. He was the son of Ambrose Bourne, a prominent pioneer Baptist minister.

By strange coincidence, Rev. Ambrose Bourne helped organize Red River Church, 1791, within a few hundred yards of where Mount Zion now stands.

Red River is one of the oldest Baptist churches

in Tennessee, and the Bourne Spring at that date, was called Prince's Spring, and the little log church building was known as Prince's meeting house. After its removal to Robertson county it took its name from its nearness to Red River. In the early days most of the churches took their names from the streams nearest which they were located, as Spring Creek, West Fork, Red River, etc. Rev. Horace Carr named the church he loved so well, from the New Testament. Hebrews 12: 22, in which Moses said, "But ye are come unto Mount Zion, and unto the city of the living God, the heavenly Jerusalem." etc.

CHAPTER V

"THE MAN WHO SPEAKS, MAY, IF HIS MESSAGE
IS GREAT ENOUGH, AND GREATLY DELIVERED, RANK
ABOVE THE RULERS OF HIS TIME."

It seems that a love for the ministry, was
inherent in the Carr family, and it is also a noticeable fact, that few, if any of them, have departed
from the Baptist faith; beginning with Uncle
Horace, and descending to his two sons, Altheus
and William, on down to his grandson, Rev.
Thomas Carr, of Kansas, son of the late Calvin
Carr, of Cheatham county.

Altheus, the fourth son of Uncle Horace, and
Aunt Kitty, was born near Port Royal, Tenn., in
the early 50's. He was obedient to his parents
from his early childhood.

While a day laborer on the farms around Port
Royal, he manifested a thirst for knowledge, and
while his plow team rested their noon hours rest,
he was not idle. He could be seen lying around

under the shade trees, either with a book in his hand or a pencil and paper.

By saving his wages, and receiving financial aid from friends, he was enabled to take a theo logical course at Fisk's University, Nashville, Tenn.

He was a negro of commanding appearance, and polite address, and after the death of his father, September, 1877, he was pastor of Mount Zion Church continuously for nine years. In his early twenties he was married to Miss Lou Gaines, daughter of Aunt Eliza Gaines, of whom I shall speak later.

After his marriage, he purchased five acres of land adjoining the Mount Zion lot, on which he built a comfortable three room cottage. It was here that he and his thrifty wife raised a large and interesting family of seven daughters, all of whom died young.

In his cottage he had his private study, in which he prepared some very able sermons, and after he thought he had his subjects well in hand, he often went to a valley near his home, on Sulphur Fork Creek, and delivered them, with the fine old elms and sycamores his silent listeners.

His funeral orations were hard to beat, several of which I had the pleasure of hearing. The first being that of William Northington, the trusted foreman for years on Miss Ellen Yates' farm. William was highly esteemed as a colored citizen of the community, and Miss Ellen sent out for her white friends to attend his funeral. They occupied seats on the back porch, while the colored congregation sat under the shade of the tall locust trees, and listened with rapt attention. After taking his text, and making a few appropriate introductory remarks, he quoted effectively from Longfellow's Psalm of Life:

"Art is long, and time is fleeting,
    And our hearts, though stout and brave,
Still, like muffled drums are beating
    Funeral marches to the grave."

William and Jack Northington were brothers, owned by Mr. Henry Northington, one of the pioneer settlers of Middle Tennessee.

Mr. Northington was a large slave owner, and not needing William and Jack on his farm, he kept them hired out.

After they were freed, they said, "We will go back to the old home, and help take care of Mars Henry the remainder of his days," and they did. Mr. Northington died June, 1877, but they still stayed on the old plantation, working as long as they lived for Miss Ellen Yates, Mr. Northington's adopted niece.

Two summers later, August, 1883, I heard him preach the funeral of Aunt Lucy Parks Northington. For several years before her death, Aunt Lucy had cooked for Mrs. Lawson Fort. She had been a faithrul servant in the Dancy, Parks, and Fort families all her life, originally belonging to William E. Dancy, of Florence, Ala.

She was beloved by her white people, who ten derly cared for her during the last two years of her life, in which she was unable to work. And when the last sad rites were to be paid her remains, her casket was placed on the front gallery of the pretty Fort home; white friends sat in the parlor and sitting room; the colored congregation occupied seats leading from the steps to the front gate. As Rev. Altheus Carr stood at the head of the casket, and 'neath the shadows of the imposing columns of that old colonial home, it was a scene to touch the tenderest chord of a Southern heart. On the casket was a wreath of spider lillies, that grew in a valley near the cabin home of the deceased, when she lived at the old Parks homestead near Port Royal. Every summer, for years, she had admired that lily bed at blooming time, and the writer remembered it.

He took for his text, "Well done good and faithful servant," etc., and started out by saying: "The nearness of this casket to the mansion door, and the pure white lillies that shed their fragrance over the heart that is forever still, attest the truth of my text. Yes my hearers, this means something. It speaks appreciation of a life, whose ending deserves more than a passing notice.

"Sister Lucy Parks Northington was sixty-one years of age, and forty-one years of this long span of life were spent in the Master's vineyard.

"She was a quiet worker, caring not for the praise of the world, but striving always to perform duties pleasing to the eye of Him who seeth in secret places.

"Too well I know, that my feeble words can do but scant justice to the life of such a departed sister, but I feel like we should hold high the light of such lives, that others may follow their brightness.

"My mother was often with Sister Lucy during her last days; they sang and prayed together, and she left every evidence that she was ready for the kingdom.

"Her last night on earth, she said to the friends keeping watch, 'Sing to me, sing the good old songs of Zion.' No doubt, but she, like the saints of old, wanted music to charm her last on earth, and greet her first in heaven.

"We shall miss her at the church she loved so well, but she has left her light on its altars, and if we would see her again, let us find her footprints, and follow them. They have not been blotted out. We will find them leading from her doorway to those of affliction, to the church door, or wherever her gentle spirit was needed.

"This quiet Summer's evening we will lay her tired body to rest on the hillside overlooking Red River; time for her is no more, but a home not made with hands, is hers to enjoy, though an endless Eternity."

The service was concluded with a song and prayer, after which the orderly funeral procession passed up the lane, and on down to the colored graveyard, where so many of the Fort colored people have been laid to rest.

There was a certain dignity and refinement about Rev. Altheus Carr that was noticeable, and which he manifested on occasions when white people attended his services.

As for instance, at the large baptizings which followed his successful revivals, when the good singing was especially inspiring, several emotional members of his church were in the habit of shouting, and at times, they were noisy in their demonstrations. When he realized that they had reached a limit, he usually in an undertone, spoke some kind word of admonition.

Often they understood a gesture from him, and

all would be quiet.   He wielded a subtle influence over his people that was remarkable.

It is a fact worthy of mention, that only one member was publicly known to rebel at the new rules set up in Mount Zion church after his became its pastor.

His father, during his nine years charge of the church, had accepted for his services only what the members saw fit to pay him.   His idea being that God did not intend for a price to be set on the preaching of the Gospel.

Neither did he advocate, or allow, church suppers as a means of raising funds for religious purposes.

But the world moves, and church conditions forced his successors to adopt new methods.

Altheus being the first to follow his father, was forced to have systematic means of raising church money, by assessing the members according to their supposed financial ability. Uncle Arter Northington, a reasonably prosperous colored tenant living on Mr. Felix Northington's premises, was assessed $2.00.

He thought it was too much, and appealed to his employer, in whose sense of right and justice he had great confidence.   The latter told him he thought fifty cents would be enough.

When the contribution box was handed round

on the next collection day, Uncle Arter dropped in his fifty cents. After preaching was over, Rev. Carr approached him privately, and quoted appropriately from Paul regarding certain religious obligations.

Uncle Arter was very black, very positive, and talked through his nose. Straightening himself up, he spoke defiantly, and said: "Brer Carr, I keers nothin' 'tall 'bout what PAUL said. Mars Felix is smart enough for ME ter go by, an he says fifty cents is plenty fer me ter pay, an that's all I'm gwine ter pay."

The incident was related at the village store, and in a spirit of amusement some one exclaimed, "Hurrah for Paul!" and from that time on, till his death, twenty-five or thirty years afterwards, Uncle Arter was known far and wide as "Paul."

CHAPTER VI.

"HE HAD AN EAR THAT CAUGHT, AND A MEMORY
THAT KEPT."

Uncle Horace was spending several days in our neighborhood, filling a whitewashing contract. Red River was past fording; he worked till late, and did not wish to risk the ferry after dark, so he "took time about," as he called it, staving among the neighbors at night.

The night he spent on my father's premises, I went after supper to Aunt Lucy's house in the back yard, and asked him to tell me of a corn shucking before the war. He drew his chair up near the door, and began as follows:

"I think about the biggest corn shucking I ever went to was on Mr. Waters' farm, between Mr. Billie Weatherford's and Mr. John Powers'. Mr. Waters was a prosperous farmer, and a mighty fine man with it.

"It was about the last of November, and the corn was piled high in a lot back of the house.

47

I would suppose there were about fifty hands invited, white and colored. They went to work, and they worked, too, I tell you.

"Old gray headed men were invited, not to work, mind you, but to sit off to themselves and talk over good old times.

"The night was cool, and frosty, and a log fire was built for their benefit. What we called the best men of the county were there. Mr. Hatcher, Mr. Hiter, Mr. Wilcox, Mr. Thomas Shaw, Mr. John Powers, and Mr. Patrick McGowan. I remember Mr. McGowan and Mr. Shaw seemed to be particular friends. They came together and went away together.

Mr. McGowan owned a yellow man named" John, and he could beat anybody there shucking corn; he could also find more red ears than anybody else, and would laugh the merriest laughs when he found them, for a red ear meant an extra dram, you know. Some of the hands accused him of bringing along a few from Mr. McGowan's corn crib, but I hardly think that was true, for when it came to honesty, John was as straight as a shingle.

"Charles, Mr. Waters' wagoner, was the heap walker that night. Always at corn shuckings they picked out somebody with a clear, good voice to sing, and made them the heap walker.

He walked over and around the corn heap, and sang the corn song. Somehow, the hands seemed to forget they worked. when thev sang, the time passed so pleasantly.

"Charles was what they called a quick witted smart fellow, and he could fit into his songs some of the funny sayings of the neighborhood, and make the people laugh amazingly. He would sing the verses alone, and the crowd would join in the chorus. The corn song went like this:

"Ginn erway de corn boys, ginn erway de corn,
  Done come here ternight, fer ter ginn erwav de corn.
  Corn, *cor*-n, *cor*-n, *cor*-n, corn fer de
  Bell cow, corn fer de mule,
  Ash cake fer de yaller gal,
  Dat make you all er fool,
Corn, corn, corn, dear old Marser's corn.'

"Then the chorus went:

'Cor-n, cor-n, ginn erway de corn
Gwine ter shuck it all dis night,
As sho's yer bor-n, bor-n.'

"And bless your life, they were happy times, those good old corn shucking davs before the war! Along about midnight, they changed up from the corn song to the dram song, and when that started up, the boys worked like steam

engines. As well as I can remember, here's the
way the dram song went:

Dram, dram, little drop er dram sir,
Dram, dram, fetch erlong de dram.
Come, come, little Mister Whiskey,
Nigger mighty thirstv, wants er little dram.'

*   *   *   *   *   *   *

"When the corn pile was finished up, Mr. Waters
took off his hat, made a polite bow, and thanked
the hands for their good work.

"Then he said: 'I'll give you something to warm
up your throats,' and hands the big jug around;
but he had good judgment, and would not give
them enough to make them drunk. When the
last one had taken his dram, John McGowan, that
same active yellow man, and one of the Sale
colored boys, caught Mr. Waters up on their
shoulders, and away they went to the house with
him, the hands following behind, singing thecorn
song. They set him down on the front door
steps.

Mrs. Waters was out in the hall, and said she
had not laughed as much sidce Christmas. We
were invited out to the big log kitchen, and there
on a long table was spread the feast of all feasts.
Boiled ham, barbecued shoat, sweet potatoes,
coffee, pumpkin pies, ginger cakes, and cider; and

50

when the supper was over, the young folks lit in to dancing. I didn't care for dancing myself, so I sat around and talked to the sober-minded folks.

"It was an old saying, that day must never break on a corn shucking feast, or bad luck would fall on the next one. So before we broke up, the boys took Mr. Waters on their shoulders three times around the house, to the music of a good bye song. Just now I can't exactly remember how that went, but it was a pretty tune.

'When we scattered out, each one going to his home, some up the road, down the road, and across the fields, the frosty night air rang with 'Run, nigger run, patroler'l ketch you,' etc.

"Of course I went to many other corn shucking frolics, but this one was the biggest I ever attended, not only this, but they had the best order I ever noticed.

"Well I've told you about a corn shucking before the war, and the next time I come back I'll tell you of when the stars fell."

"Tell me now," I said, "something may happen that you will not come again soon; its not late, and you will have time to tell part of it any way."

He looked serious and said, "Well I was not to say *skeered*, but it was certainly a solemn time! I was twenty-one years old when it happened, and was sleeping up stairs in a cabin on Miss Nancy Carr's farm. A pitiful noise waked me, and I bounced up and run down, and the wood-pile in front of the cabin door was full of stars!

"I said, '*signs and wonders in the heavens*"

"Mr. Bob Bellamy, from Kentucky, was working at Miss Nancy's, and he seemed to think it was funny, the way the colored people prayed and shouted, thinking judgment day was at hand. We could hear them praying at Mr. Riah Grant's home, as plain as if they were in our yard.

"Brother Martin Grant was a colored preacher, and a mighty good man; he tried to reason with them, and told them they were in the hands of the Lord, and He would deal right with them.

"The white folks did not seem to be much excited. The very religious ones prayed in secret, but they made no great noise; the excitement was mostly among the colored people, and the ignorant white folks.

"After daybreak, and it began to get light, the stars on the ground grew dim, and got dimmer, and dimmer, till the sun came up and they could not be seen at all. An old colored man living down on the Clarksville road rejoiced when he saw the sun rise, and said, 'Thank God, I know the world is all right now, for the sun is rising in the same place!'

"I think Brother Robin Northington (at that time a young man belonging to Mr. David Northington) made more noise than any colored person in the neighborhood. In his young days he was inclined to be wild, and when he thought judgment day had found him unprepared, it was time to make a noise.

"It always seemed strange to me that Brother Robin was so late coming into the church. He was eighty odd, when he joined Mount Zion last year."

*   *   *   *   *   *   *

The writer witnessed Uncle Robin's baptism in Sulphur Fork Creek, near Mount Zion Church; there were eighty candidates for baptism, and Uncle Horace had his son Altheus to perform the sacred rite.

On account of Uncle Robin's advanced age, and a very remarkable experience he had related the day he joined the church, he seemed to be a central figure of the occasion, and all eyes were turned on him, as he stood trembling at the water's edge, pleading, "Now Brer Carr, be perticular, and *don't* you *droun* me!"

"Be quiet Brother Northington," he said in his

characteristic dignified tone, "by the help of the Lord I will take you safely through; Brother Edwards and Brother Baldrv are here to assist me and you need not fear."

It was soon over, and his nervousness gave place to rejoicing. I don't think I ever heard sweeter singing than went up from hundreds of colored worshippers on the hillsides surrounding Mount Zion Church, that lovely Sabbath morning, October, 1875.

CHAPTER VII.

"ITS A GRAND THING TO MAKE SOMETHING OUT OF THE LIFE GOD HATH GIVEN US, BUT IT IS GRANDER STILL, TO REACH THE GREAT END OVER GREAT DIFFICULTIES."

James William Carr, the twelfth, and next to the youngest child of Uncle Horace, and Aunt Kitty, attained distinction both as a lecturer and a minister.

A Tennessean by birth, and a Georgian by Providence, he died in the midst of his usefulness at Savannah, Ga., August 25, 1907.

In his youth, he professed religion and joined Mount Zion during his father's pastorate of the church. His early educational advantages were poor, but he was ambitious, and lost no opportunity for mental improvement.

Rev. William Carr was tall, and bright colored, having his mother's refined features, and his father's good physique.

A blend of both parents in looks, and Christian principles.

That he was appreciative, the following letter received by the writer, a short time before his death, will show:

SAVANNAH, GA., May 13, 1907.

"*Mrs. J. F. Miller*—Kind Friend: Today my thoughts go back to the scenes of my boyhood, away back in the 70's, when I worked for your father. How well do I remember the day he hired me, and carried me home behind him, on a big sorrel horse he called Charlie.

"I had never lived with white people, and Mother Kitty did not think I would be satisfied, but I was, and stayed several months, going home every Saturday evening.

"I date my start in life to the study table in your father's family room at night, around which I was not only permitted the use of books, but was also instructed in them.

"One day I ventured to ask you to set me some copies, in a rude copy book I had pinned together of foolscap paper. You asked if I wanted words, or sentences. I was embarrassed, for I did not know the difference, and you set both.

"I feel profoundly grateful to you, and your family, for the interest manifested in the little yellow boy from near Horse Shoe Bend.

"I have traveled from the Atlantic to the Pacific, and from Lake Michigan to the Gulf of

56

Rev. John William Carr, Savannah, Ga.

Mexico, and I have been treated with respect wherever I have gone.

"I am at present pastor of the First African Baptist Church of Savannah. It was organized in 1788. The membership is 5,000, and the value of the church property, $100,000.00. This church has had only six pastors during its existence of 119 years; I am its sixth.

"The race riot in Atlanta a few months ago, has in no way changed my opinion of the South as being the proper home of the negro.

"I am glad you visited my mother, and took down in writing some interesting incidents of her life.

"My parents were unlettered it is true, for their sphere was limited, but our Heavenly Father can be glorified in little things as well as great things.

"It matters not how small the deed of kindness done, it is the motive that dignifies the action.

"Providence permitting, I hope to visit Port Royal next fall, and meet once more in the flesh my friends and kindred there. If I come I will preach a sermon or two at Mount Zion. It is a dear old church to me, and the quiet spot near by, in which sleeps the dust of my father and two brothers, is dearer still.

"May God's richest blessings rest on your household, is the prayer of,

Your obedient servant,

J. W. CARR.

*　　*　　*　　*　　*　　*　　*

In three months after the above letter was written, Rev. William Carr was stricken with fever and died. The news of his death was telegraphed to his only surviving brother, Horace Carr, of District No. 1, Montgomery county, Tenn.

Immediately following this, memorial services were held in several Middle Tennessee and Southern Kentucky churches in which he had preached before making Savannah his home.

Deceased was twice married. His second wife and several children survive him.

Apropos of Rev. William Carr's reference to the First African Baptist Church at Savannah, I quote the following from an article in the *Informer*, written by Wm. L. Craft (col.), Field Secretary of the National B. Y. P. U. Board, Nashville, Tennessee:

"The colored Baptists of the United States have cause to feel proud of the results of their distinctive organic church work within the past 120 years.

And to the State of Georgia we owe it, to call

her the Mother State of negro organic church life.

"It was in Savannah, January 20, 1788, that the first negro Baptist church was organized by Rev. Andrew Bryan, and numerous other slaves converted under his earnest preaching.

"Rev. Bryan was converted under the preaching of Rev. George Leile, and baptized, 1783, in the Savannah River. At the close of the Civil War, 1865, there were 400,000 negro Baptists in the United States.

"Today they are estimated at 3,000,000, and well organized. The National Colored Baptist Convention was organized at Montgomery, Ala., in 1880, and shows 89 State Conventions; 559 Associations; 18,214 churches; 17,217 ordained ministers; 15,625 Sunday Schools; 73,172 officers and teachers; 788,016 pupils.

"The officers of this National Convention are as follows: Rev. E. C. Morris, D. D., Helena, Ark., President; Prof. R. B. Hudson, A. M., Selma, Ala., Recording Secretary; Rev. A. J. Stokes, D. D., Montgomery, Ala., Treasurer; Rev. Robert Mitchell, A. M., D. D., Bowling Green, Ky., Auditor; Rev. S. W. Bacote, D. D., Statistician.

"The work of this great body is conducted by National Boards, under the management of Corresponding Secretaries.

"The denominational organ speaking for this Convention, is *The National Baptist Union*, published weekly at Nashville, Tenn. E. W. D Isaac, D. D., is editor, and said to be one of the ablest in the United States."

It was in a speech made on Georgia soil, that first gave Booker T. Washington the eve and ear of the Nation, when he said, "It is worth far more to the negro to have the privilege of making an honest dollar side by side with the white man, than it is to have the privilege of spending that dollar sitting by him in a theatre." It is this wholesome doctrine that has given him the right influence among right thinking people of both races.

When Booker Washington left Hampton Insti tute, Virginia, that great school for the practical training of the negro, he began his life work at a country cross roads, near Tuskegee, Alabama. It proved a good stopping place for that young and penniless, but cultured son of Hampton Institute.

As an educator and civic builder, he is known and honored wherever the forces of Christian civilization recount their worthies, and crown their heroes. It is a remarkable record, that in all his utterances, on both sides of the sea, Booker Washington has never been known to say a foolish or intemperate thing.

Speaking further of Georgia, it is asserted on good authority that the negroes of this State pay taxes on something over $18,000,000 worth of property. It is property at last, that is the test of civilized citizenship, especially in a land where good men may readily attain it.

With whiskey out of the reach of a race having a lamentable weakness for it. it is highly probable that these figures will be greatly increased within the next decade. The truth is gradually becoming known to the world, that the South is giving to the negro the only square deal a white race ever gave to one of another color, living among them under the same laws.

Through the refining influence of the holy teachings of the Man of Galilee, the Southern white man is harmonizing with his "Brothers in Black," to a degree that he is spending three hundred million dollars in their education; not only this, but he is supplying them with wealth accumulating work, and allowing them to enjoy the rights of peaceable citizenship. That they duly appreciate all this, is daily expressed in the right living of the best element of our colored population.

CHAPTER VIII.

In the preparation of this little book, it has been my earnest desire to secure my information from reliable sources, and. so far, I think I have succeeded in doing so.

After writing the preceding chapters, it occurred to me that I would like to read them to some member of the Carr family, before giving them to the public. So Rev. Luke Fort, of Guthrie, Ky., came to my home, May 13, 1911, and spent a good portion of the day.

Rev. Fort, in antebellum times, belonged to Mr. Lawson Fort, He is sixty-four years of age, and the most of his useful life was spent on the Fort plantation. He was married during the 70's to Annie, youngest daughter of Uncle Horace and Aunt Kitty Carr.

Rev. Fort not only endorsed as correct what had already been written, but he gave me additional information that I consider both valuable and interesting. He spoke in part as follows:

"When I first heard that you wished to talk to me of a family I loved so well, I was afraid I could be of but little assistance to you, but after hearing you read what had already been written my mind was awakened, and the old scenes came back to me.

"I was the son-in-law of these dear old people nineteen years, and twelve years of that time, (after Father Horace's death) Mother Kitty lived with me.

"It was while I was a tenant on Mr. W. D. Fort's farm. After the day's work was done, we used to gather around the fireside in winter, or on the front porch in Summer, and listen to her talk. Everybody liked to hear her talk. But after she broke up housekeeping and had no cares, if possible, she seemed more interesting than at any period of her life. My regret is, that I did not take more note of what she said.

"Her theme was religion, for she was an every day Christian. During her widowhood, she went to live awhile with her son, William, who was at that time living at Indianapolis Indiana, but-she was not satisfied, and soon returned to Tennessee. At her advanced age, she could not get used to the great difference between town and country life."

From Aunt Kitty we turned to Uncle Horace, and Rev. Fort continued:

"Father Horace had his own peculiar style of preaching, and often his sermons would be made up entirely of some good religious experience he had especially enjoyed.

"He was partial to the Gospel of John, and the best sermon I ever heard him preach was from the 15th chapter and 1st verse, 'I am the true vine, and my Father is the husbandman.' Feeling the infirmities of old age coming on, and knowing that Altheus had chosen the ministry, he often put him to the front in the pulpit, while he sat back, in his humble way, and directed the service. While sitting beneath the sound of his voice, in Scriptural language he doubtless thought to himself, 'This is my son, in whom I am well pleased.' He seemed to be getting ready for Altheus to step into his shoes, and carry on the good work he had begun. The foundation had been laid."

Rev. Fort then paid fine tribute to the memories of his white people, Mr. Lawson Fort, and his pious wife. To the latter he said he owed his first religious impressions. When a mere boy waiting about the house, she talked to him of salvation in a way that he understood, and he

Rev. Luke Fort, Guthrie, Ky.

was led to trust his Savior at an early age. And after he was a middle aged man, she often invited him to attend devotional exercises in the seclusion of her family room; on one accasion she requested him to lead in prayer, which he did.

Never having heard of the colored meetings held on the Fort plantation before the war, only in a general way, I asked Rev. Luke Fort if he remembered one, and he said he did, very distinctly. It was during the middle 50's when he was about seven years old. It was Saturday night, and the first time he ever heard Uncle Horace preach

The service was held in what they called Aunt Margaret's house, a large, comfortable log room, with a shed at one end, and an upstairs. There were two doors in the main room, opposite each other, and facing east and west. Along between ten and eleven, o'clock the meeting reached its most enjoyable stage. The good old time songs were making their souls happy. Uncle Horace led the songs, and his face wore that placid look that seemed to speak that no wave of trouble would ever roll across his peaceful breast," when a rap was heard at the front door. and before they had time to think, in rushed a band of patrolers!

As they came in at the east door, the confused

congregation made hasty exit from the west door.

The news was quickly conveyed to the kind old master, who sent his son, the late Sugg Fort, to the scene of excitement. Young Mr. Fort approached the patrolers in a very dignified manner, and informed them that his father had sent him to tell them that their services were not needed on his premises. It was before the county line had been changed, Mr. Fort's residence was then in Montgomery county, instead of Robertson, its present location, and the patrolers were from Port Royal.

(For the benefit of a younger generation of readers, I will state that patrolers were organized bands of white men, appointed in each neighborhood, for the purpose of going about at night and keeping order among a doubtful element of colored people who left home without passes, or written permission from their owners. The unfortunate condition of affairs demanded it, and still more unfortunate was it, that the appointment, or office, too often fell into cruel and inhuman hands.)

There lived at Port Royal, a fine looking colored man by the name of Dean Dancy, the property of the late John A. Dancy. It so happened that Dean was masquerading this particular Saturday night without a pass, and unluckily fell into the hands of the patrolers. Knowing they would deal roughly with him under such circumstances, he compromised the matter by telling them, if they'd let him off just this one time, he'd pilot them to a negro meeting, where they could find a housefull of people without passes, and this was why Uncle Horace's meeting was so disturbed.

Monday morning Mr. Fort ordered his saddle horse brought out unusually early; he rode over to Port Ropal and informed Mr. Dancy of what his boy Dean had done, and the trickster had to make some pretty fair promises to escape punishment.

On the same night that Dean Dancy led the patrolers to molest the quiet worshipers on Mr. Fort's plantation, an amusing scene was enacted in a dry goods store at Port Royal. It was during the late fall, and several of the village clerks had put up a notice that they would pay liberally for a fat, well cooked o'possum, delivered at Dancy and Kirby's store. Joe Gaines, a tall brown skinned man belonging to W. N. Gaines, gleaned the persimmon trees round about the Gaines premises, and failing to find an o'possum, conceived the idea of substituting a fat house-cat. After it was nicely cooked, he stepped out by the light of the moon, with his pass in his pocket, and hope in his heart of bringing back a silver dollar.

The clerks from the other business houses assembled at Dancy and Kirby's, where a spread was set for eight o possum eaters. Dr. J. T. Darden a young physician from Turnersville, had a short time before located at Port Royal, and was invited to the feast. When the dish containing the supposed delectable marsupial was uncovered, it was observed that the young physician began to view it with a suspicious eye. He called Mr. T. M. Kirby to one side and told him the carcass was not that of an o'possum and thev must not eat it. Upon closer examination it was very plain that it was a cat.

Without a word, Mr. Dancy walked to the front door and turned the key, locking them in; a pistol was placed on the table, and Joe was informed that he must devour that cat, or suffer the consequences.

It required the effort of his life, but he choked it down. If Dean and Joe ever had good intentions, Satan certainly run rough shod over them all that Saturday night.

*   *   *   *   *   *   *

Along with the progress of colored churches within the past four decades, that of orders, and societies is worthy of mention.

Within a short distance of each other, thev have, near Port Royal, both Odd Fellows and

Benevolent Society halls. Of the latter society I shall speak more in detail, from the fact that it is much older as an organization, in this community, and has done so much for its members. It was organized, October, 1872, in a little log school room, on what was called Sugar Camp Branch, on Miss Ellen Yates' farm.

Dennis Neblett, a good colored man of that vicinity, was the prime mover in the enterprise, and called to his assistance in its organization Granville Wilcox and Henry Roberts (col.), of Clarksville, Tenn.

They organized with thirty charter members, and Dennis Neblett was elected President, which office he faithfully filled for thirty-seven years.

This feeble but faithful little band met three years in Sugar Camp Branch school room, after which the house was moved farther down the creek, on Mr. Henry Rosson's farm. Being too remote from the majority of its members, they lost interest and failed to attend the meetings as they had formerly done, so the officers adopted the plan of meeting in the homes of the members, and occasionally at the churches.

The change awakened renewed interest, and from that time on, it gradually increased from thirty members to something near one hundred and fifty. Its noble mission is to assist the disabled, nurse the sick, and bury the dead.

In the early 90's they bought a lot on the principal street of Port Royal, on which they erected a very modest little hall They were fortunate in making this investment at that date, as the remainder of their treasury, $200.00 (two hundred) deposited in a Clarksville bank, was lost during the failure of several banks at that time in Clarksville. After meeting at Port Royal lodge a number of years, they decided to purchase a more suitable location. The old Carr home near Port Royal had been dismantled, and the land was bought by Mr. Joshua Ford, a prosperous farmer of District No. 5, Montgomery county. Mr. Ford disposed of his purchase in lots, Jerry Fort (col.) being the first purchaser of five acres, on which he built a comfortable little home.

Jerry and Harry Grant, as Trustees for the Benevolent Society, were appointed to purchase three acres of the same tract, adjoining his, for a burying ground, and also a parade ground for the society. The purchase was made, but afterward sold for residence lots, now owned and occupied by Jane Davis. Lecie Hollins and George Watson.

A large tobacco barn on the opposite side of the road, fronting the Fort home, had been used for several years as a shelter for the society when the members gave barbecues and other out-door festivities. This barn, including one-quarter of an acre, was bought by the Trustees, the building sold to Sim Polk (col.) and moved to his farm on Parson's Creek, and a nice Hall, Benevolent Treasure No. 7, erected on the site, at a cost of something less than a thousand dollars. This building speaks well for its enterprising members, and is an ornament to the roadside.

Added to the membership, is a juvenile branch of the order, consisting of about fifty polite boys and girls, ranging from four to sixteen years of age.

In its first organization, 1872, this society was known as Benevolent Society No. 3, but a few years ago changed conditions made it necessary to reorganize, after which it was called Benevolent Treasure No. 7. Its present officers are as follows:

Sim Polk, President.

John Person, Vice-President.

George Watson, Recording Secretary.

Wavmond Polk, Assistant Secretary.

Harry Grant, Treasurer.

Willis Northington, Chaplain.

Wright Watkins, Lizzie Dortch, Chairmen of Sick Committee.

Demps Trabue, Chairman Executive Committee.

The meetings are held semi-monthly.

CHAPTER IX.

To the aged, it is a delightful refuge. I found this especially true in the case of Aunt Gaines Williams, whom I visited May 16, 1911

She was living with her youngest daughter, Mrs. Sarah Northington, on Esq. James'H. Achey's farm. Not until I began, several years ago, to interview these faithful old colored representatives of antebellum times, did I know how their minds were stored with rich recollections.

I was anxious to talk with Aunt Eliza, because she had been in touch with the Carr family all her life, and her daughter had been the wife of the late Rev. Altheus Carr.

Aunt Eliza was born in 1828, as the property of Major James Norfleet, a prominent citizen of Robertson county, who owned large possessions on Sulphur Fork Creek; his homestead site being now owned by Greer Brothers, a mile or two

Aunt Eliza Gaines—Williams.   Mother of five
generations of her family.

son; their oldest daughter, Margaret, married Gabe Washington, and their daughter, Amanda, has grand-children. While I was talking about my white folks, I forgot to tell you they were kin to the 'big folks,' the Bakers, the Dortch's, and Governor Blount. These three families lived out on Parson's Creek, and Major Baker gave the land on his place for that great camp ground, called Baker's Camp Ground. Lor, the good old times the people used to have at the Baker's camp meetings. You could hear them shouting for miles! The little church wasn't much larger than a family room, but they had tents all along the creek bottom near the big Baker spring, and held the meetings two or three weeks at a time. Brother Horace Carr enjoyed these camp meetings; I've heard him tell of some of the big sermons old Dr. Hanner, Dr. West, and others used to preach there, but somehow he was partial to Red River Church, above all the rest. It was through his influence that I, and a host of others joined Red River, and then when we were freed, and the Lord blessed us with a church of our own, we followed him to Mount Zion.

"If everybody that Brother Horace influenced to be Christians here on earth are with him in heaven today, he has a glorious throng around him. I will never forget the last time I saw southeast of Port Royal. At her birth, Major Norfleet gave her to his daughter Louisa, who named her for a favorite schoolmate, Mary Eliza Wheatley, but for short they always called her Eliza. Her mind seemed to dwell first, on her white people, of whom she spoke as follows:

"My young Mistress, Miss Louisa Norfleet, married Mr. Abraham Gaines, Mr. Billie Gaines' father, and lived where Mr. Ed. Bourne now lives, in the village of Port Royal. When Mr. Billie Gaines was a few months old his mother went to Mr. Sam Northington's to spend a few days, and while she was there she ate something that disagreed with her, and died suddenly from congestion of the stomach.

"I had a baby child nearly the same age of hers, and I nursed them both at my own breast. That has been sixty odd years ago, but I grieve for her till yet, for she was good to me. I'm trying to be ready to meet her. Mr. Billie Gaines does not forget me; he comes to see me, and sends me a present now and then, and so does Mr. Frazier Northington.

"I was the mother of fourteen children by my first husband, Wiley Gaines, and there is something in my family that very few people live to see, the fifth generation. My oldest daughter, Annie, married Henry Fort, Sister Margaret Fort's him. I heard he was sick, and I went over and carried him a lunch basket of nice things to eat. The weather was warm, and he was able to bring his chair out and sit in his yard. He had dropsy and did not live very long after that. He talked of heaven most of the time; he would clap his hands and say:

'I'm nearing my Father's house,
  Where many mansions be,
Nearer the great white throne,
  My people are waiting for me.'

"I used to go to Brother Horace's prayer meetings that he held around at night in homes that permitted him, and one night he called on me to pray in public. I was confused, and did not say but a few words, but he told me that a few from the heart were worth ten thousand from the tongue. When I told him good bye, the last visit I made him, he held my hand a long time, and pointed toward heaven and said, 'In the name of our Lord, we must set up our banner. Set it high, and never look down.'"

*   *   *   *   *   *   *

After the first talk with Aunt Eliza, I made a second visit, the same week, for the purpose of taking her picture, but after reaching her home a rain storm came on suddenly, and we could not get the sunlight necessary to picture making. She had peen advised by telephone that we would be there, and was nicely dressed for the occasion. Strange to say, she was eighty-two years old, and had never had a picture taken.

We succeeded next day however, in securing a very good one.

On my second visit to her she met me at the door in her characteristic pleasant manner and said:

"I've been studying a heap about what you said and read to me the other evening when you were here, and I told my daughter that I believed the Lord had directed you to write this history of my people, and their early struggles. If somebody does not take it up, the old heads will all soon be gone, and there will be nobody left to tell the story."

Among the older members of Mount Zion Church who have aided me materially in securing facts concerning its early history, I would mention Dan and Jerry Fort. While neither of them were charter members, they have been prominently identified with the church for many years. They have seen it rise from the little box house, with its seventy unlettered members of forty-three years ago, to a reasonably well educated mem- bership of something over three hundred.

Crude and humble as that first church building was, I have heard it said that Uncle Horace on preaching days would pause on the hillside before entering, and praise God for the privileges he enjoyed. It seemed that a new heart was in his bosom and a new song was on his lips. He loved the little house of worship as though it had been handed down to him as a present, direct from heaven.

Uncle Horace was instrumental in organizing two other churches besides Mount Zion, Antioch, near Turnersville, in Robertson county, and Nevil's Chapel, near Rudolphtown, in Montgomery. Along with prominent mention of the great Christian leader of his people, I must not omit due tribute to some of his followers; principal among whom was Uncle John McGowan, a member of Mount Zion Church forty-two years, and all the time leading a life worthy of emulation.

Uncle John was born on what was known as the George Wimberly place near Rossview, in Montgomery county, in 1822. He was the property of Miss Katherine Wimberly, who married Mr. Milton Bourne, brother of the late Mr. William Bourne, of Port Royal, Tenn. Mr. Milton Bourne owned and settled the present homestead site of Mr. John Gower, of Port Royal. After living happily there for a number of years, he became financially embarrassed, and was forced to sell some of his most valuable slaves. Among them, in young manhood's prime, was Uncle John, who, in no spirit of bitterness, often referred to his sale as follows: "A large block, or box, was placed in the front yard for us to stand on, that the bidders might get a good look at us. The bid opened lively when I was put up, for I was considered a pretty likely man, as the saying went. When the bidding went way up into several hundred dollars, I was knocked off to Mr. Lawson Fort. I was glad of that, for I had lived near him and knew him to be a good man. I hadn't long settled my mind down on having a good home the balance of my life, when up comes somebody and told me Mr. Fort didn't buy me, he was just bidding for Mr. Patrick McGowan. 'My feathers fell,' as the saying is, for I didn't know how me and an Irishman I didn't know anything about were going to get along together. But it so happened that we got along fine; while his ways were a little different from what I had been used to with Mr. Bourne and the Wimberleys, I soon found him to be a man that would treat you right if you deserved it. He had his own curious way of farming, and no matter what price was paid for tobacco, he would not let a plant grow on his place. He had a very good little farm joining the Royster place, and raised more potatoes than anybody in that whole country.

"I have heard him tell often of letting Elder Reuben Ross, the great Baptist preacher that came to this country from North Carolina over a hundred years ago, live in a cabin in his yard till he could arrange to get a better home. Elder Ross had a large family, and Mr. McGowan took some of them in his own house. He was kind to strangers, and never turned the needy from his door.

"I must tell you of a whipping I got while I belonged to Mr. Milton Bourne, that I did not deserve, and if I had the time to go over again, I would whip the negro who caused me to get it. There was a still house on Red River, not far from Mr. Sugg Fort's mill, it was long before Mr. Fort owned the mill; Mr. Joe Wimberly owned and operated the stillhouse. In that day and time, the best people of the land made whiskey; it was pure, honest whiskey, and did not make those who drank it do mean things, like the whiskey of today. Mr. Bourne had hired me to Mr. Wimberly to work in the still house, with a lot of other boys, about my age—along about nineteen and twenty years old. We were a lively set of youngsters, and laid a plan to steal a widow woman's chickens one night and have a chicken fry. We took a solemn pledge just before we started, that we would never 'tell on each other, if the old lady suspicioned us. Well we stole them, and one of the boys, Bob Herndon, who had been raised to help his mammy about the kitchen, was a pretty good cook, and he fried them. I think it was the best fried chicken I ever put in my mouth. A day or two went by, the still house shut down, and they put me to work in the field. Corn was knee high, I was chopping out bushes in a field near the river, when I saw Mr. Wimberly's overseer come stepping down the turn row like he was mad as a hornet. I knew him so well, I could tell when he was mad, as far as I could see him. My heart began to beat pretty fast, as he asked about the chickens. I told him I did not know a thing about them, but when he began to tell things that really took place, I knew some one had given us away. He got out his rope and tied me to a hickory sapling, and said: 'Now John, I'm going to give you a little dressing off for this, Bob Herndon has let the cat out of the wallet; of course he is the biggest rascal of the gang.' Every now and then he'd stop, and ask me if I was ready to own up, but he soon found I was not, and turned me loose to chopping bushes out of the corn again. About twenty years after that, I met that same

Uncle John McGowan, the great Broom Maker.

overseer at the mill one rainy day; he was older, and I reckon his heart had softened, and we laughed and talked over that chicken fry, and what it cost me. It was the first and last dishonorable scrape I ever got into."

Uncle John was twice married, and the father of several highly respected sons, and daughters, several of whom still survive him. His second son by his first marriage, Rev. Burnett McGowan, is a Baptist minister of some prominence, and owns a nice little home near Adams, Tennessee. Uncle John was an expert broom maker, and during the last twenty years of his life he made a circuit of certain sections of Robertson and Montgomery counties about three times a year, delivering his brooms to his old customers, who would use no other make but "The John McGowan brand." They were honest brooms, and lasted twice as long as the factory made ones. He had a business way of distributing broom corn seed among his customers at planting time, and after the corn was harvested, he would follow the crops, and make up the brooms on the shares.

He was so polite and pleasant that his friends, both white and colored, made him welcome in their homes free of charge, a week or ten days at a time during the broom making season. He was a fine judge of human nature, and often discussed in a very original manner the characteristics of the families with whom he stayed. After a short illness from the infirmities of old age, he died at the home of his son, Rev. Burnett McGowan, August, 1910. He was laid to rest at the old E. L. Fort homestead, with impressive ceremonies by Benevolent Treasure Lodge No. 7, of which he had long been an honored member.

CHAPTER X.

"TO LIVE IN HEARTS WE LEAVE BEHIND, IS NOT TO DIE."

Before pronouncing the benediction in this pleasant meeting with old familiar faces, I must not fail to say more of the kind old master who was as respectful to his dusky body servant as to his proudest peer, and who could penetrate color, poverty, and untutored speech, and find where a true heart lodged. Eppa Lawson Fort was born at "Riverside," a picturesque homestead on Red River, three miles southeast of Port Royal, Tennessee, August, 1802. He was the son of a prominent Baptist minister, and a church goer, but strange to say, during a pilgrimage of nearly ninety years, never joined a church. He believed implicitly in God's mercy, and when approached by friends, on the subject of religion, he would assure them that the Lord would manifest Himself to him in a way that he would understand, when He was ready for him to enter the Christian fold.

Mr. Fort was twice married, the first time to Miss Virginia Metcalfe, of Robertson county, and the second to Miss Elizabeth Dancy, of Florence, Alabama. Three sons blessed his first marriage, and a son and daughter his last, all of whom are dead. For the benefit of those of my readers who knew Mr. Fort and his last wife, I give below a brief sketch of family history:

The Forts, Dancys and Wimberlys were related, and came from North Carolina to Tennessee at an early date. The first Fort family settled on Sulphur Fork Creek, near Beech Valley Mill, at a place now owned by Mr. Plummer Poole. The Wimberlys went nearer Clarksville, on Red River and their first homestead is now occupied by their descendants, Messrs. Joe and Alf Killebrew, of Rossview neighborhood. Esq. William E. Dancy located near Dunbar's Cave, but later moved to Florence, Alabama, carrying with him a number of valuable slaves, and a family consisting of his wife and three small children, Caroline, Elizabeth and John. It was before the day of railroads, and all the visiting between the Tennessee and Alabama relatives was done on horseback, covering a period of several days' journey. During the 30's little Caroline and Elizabeth had grown to young ladyhood and accompanied by a younger brother, they came to visit the Wimberlys. They found

Mr. Fort a gay young widower, and he found Miss Elizabeth Dancy a charming young lady. A few months prior to this, he had paid his addresses to a popular young lady of Port Royal, and they were engaged, but by dint of accident he learned from a reliable source that she had said publicly that she did not intend to be bothered with his three little boys, so he frankly informed her that his children were first, and released her.

After spending several weeks in Tennessee, as the time had come for the Dancy girls to return to Alabama, Mr. Fort asked the privilege of escorting them, by saying he had not seen "Cousin Nancy," their mother, in a long time, and that she was his favorite relative. The old folks saw clearly through it all, and were pleased, and after a two weeks' visit Mr. Fort returned home, with the prospect of being their son-in-law some time during the coming year.

The three sweet little motherless boys, Jack, Ilai and Sugg, in the meantime were being tenderly cared for bv their mother's relatives. A year sped quickly by; a black broadcloth wedding suit was packed in a pair of leather saddle bags, and mounted on a handsome dappled gray horse, Mr. Fort set his face southward, with bright anticipations. A letter had preceded him, telling them what day to expect him; it was before the time of sewing machines, and the bridesmaids, Hannah and Lute Barton, had been in the Dancy home several days making the wedding dresses; they and the bride were to be dressed alike, in white muslin, flounced to the waist, and flounces bound with white satin ribbon. Esq. Dancy lived on what was known as "The Military Road," cut out by Andrew Jackson during the Creek War, and horsemen could be seen a long way off.

Toward sunset a member of the family looked up the road and exclaimed, "Yonder comes the Tennessee widower!" and they all ran out to meet him. He set his saddle bags in the hall, and incidentally mentioned their contents, whereupon the bride elect took out the broadcloth suit and neatly folded it away in a bureau drawer in her room. In those days there were no trunks, but few spare rooms, and no foolish conventionalities. Along with the clothes was a fine pair of No. 5 pump sole shoes, to be worn on the wedding occasion. Mr. Fort had a small, shapely foot, and it was said the young ladies in the Dancy home, assisting the bride in her preparation for the wedding, would go every now and then and peep admiringly at those dainty pumps in the bureau drawer.

Mr. Dancy made his daughter a bridal present of a nice black saddle horse, called "Indian," and when they turned their faces toward Tennessee, mounted on this black and white steeds, it must have been an interesting picture. Seventy odd years ago, think of the changes!

For her traveling suit, the bride wore a purple marino riding habit, made with long pointed tight waist, with hooks and eyes beneath the waist line underneath, by which it could be temporarily shortened and converted into a walking suit, thereby saving her the trouble of dressing when they took lodging at the wayside inns or taverns, as they were called. (It will be remembered that a bridal wardrobe folded in saddle pockets afforded but few dresses for change.) A shaker straw bonnet, with a green berege frill, or skirt, completed her outfit.

The headpiece of these Shaker bonnets, or "scoops," as they were called, were shaped something like the cover of an emigrant's wagon, and were anything but pleasant to wear in warm weather.

On reaching the Tennessee River, Mr. Fort's fine gray horse grew stubborn, and refused to step into the large ferry boat, and had to be blindfolded. The trip was a long and tiresome one, and the bride was laid up for repairs over a week; the scorching July sun had dealt roughly with her delicate complexion, and before she was aware of it, the back of her neck was deeply blistered from the sun shining through the thin berege skirt of her Shaker bonnet.

The faithful servants did all in their power to make her feel at home; then and there an ideal home life began, and Mr. Fort was a prime factor in making it so.

The following amusing story was often told of him: He had a nice herd of dairy cows, and among them was one they called "Stately," the bell cow. Aunt Margaret was the milk maid, and she always carried along with her to the cow pen her ten-year-old son, Nelson, "to keep the calves off," as they termed it. One summer evening about sunset, the family were seated on the front gallery, Mr. Fort, his wife, and their youngest son, the late W. D. Fort. They were quietly discussing the expected arrival next day of some favorite relatives from Paris, Texas, Dr. Joe Fort's family.

Suddenly Nelson appeared on the scene, and in breathless excitement exclaimed, "Mars Lawson, old Stately poked her head in a wagon wheel up at the lot, and she can't get it out, and mammy says what must she do about it?"

Mr. Fort sprang to his feet, and on the impulse of the moment said, "Tell one of the men up at the lot feeding, to get an axe and cut her fool

Revs. F. C. Plaster, and W. S. Adams, who assisted
in Rev. Horace Carr's ordination at Old Red
River Church, before the Civil War.

head off, QUICK!'" It was too good to keep, and his son treasured it as a household joke, which he enjoyed telling on his kind old father, along with many others equally as amusing.

But the happy old Riverside home was to undergo changes. After a few days illness, from the infirmities of old age, Mr. Fort quietly fell asleep, July 12, 1891. His remains were laid to rest with Masonic honors at the old Metcalfe burying ground on Elk Fork Creek, near Sadlersville, Tenn.

His family feasted on his affections, and his friends enjoyed the wealth of his noble nature.

*   *   *   *   *   *   *

Since the lives of most of the good people mentioned in this little story centered around Port Royal, I deem it not amiss to tell something of this historic spot.

Nearly four generations have passed since this village, which tradition tells us, lacked only one vote of being the Capitol of the State, was settled. In 1789, Samuel Wilcox, of Port Royal, South Carolina, came with his small family and settled near a large spring, on the left bank of Red River, at the foot of a ridge called "The Devil's Backbone." The exact location may be better known today by pointing the reader to a slight elevation on the far side of W. N. Gaines' bottom eld, lying between his "Hill Top" home and Sulphur Fork Creek, nearly opposite the old Weatherford mill site.

Located as he was, between Red River on the one side and Sulphur Fork Creek on the other, he soon realized his mistake, for during the high water season a vast area of this level tract, including his home, was subject to overflow.

So he crossed over Sulphur Fork Creek a few hundred yards northwest, to a picturesque point where the creek empties into Red River, and built a primitive residence, and a blacksmith shop, and called the place Port Royal, in honor of his native town in South Carolina. Mr. Wilcox later on entered about\ one thousand acres of land three or four miles from Port Royal, on the Graysville road leading to Kentucky. A portion of his original purchase is now owned by Mr. Polk Prince, of District No. 1, Montgomery county.

This was the first permanent settlement made at Port Royal. But fourteen years earlier, 1775, the historian 'tells us of tragic scenes enacted thereabouts, as follows:

"A famous hunter by the name of Manscoe, and three companions, camped a few weeks near where Sulphur Fork Creek empties into Red River, and here Manscoe had an adventure with some Indians. Having discovered from their trail, that a hunting party of some sort was in the vicinity, he went alone to ascertain if possible who they were.

"On the bank of the river, he saw a camp fire, and creeping as close as he dared, he saw two Indians, whom he recognized as belonging to the Black Feet tribe. Manscoe was about to retire to carry the news to his companions, when one of the Indians arose and came directly toward him. Manscoe fired, and the Indian wheeled and ran about fifty yards past his own camp fire and fell dead over the bluff into the river. The other Indian made quick time away from the fatal spot, not knowing, it was supposed, how many whites were in the attacking party. Manscoe not knowing the number of savages, beat a hasty retreat also. Joining his comrades, he returned in a few hours, accompanied by them, to find the fugitive Indian had, in the meantime, been to his camp, packed his scant belongings on his pony, and left for parts unknown. They followed close on his trail, the remainder of the day, but never found him.

"Knowing that the Indians would soon return in full force to avenge the death of their comrade, Manscoe and his party left the country within the next few hours, but terribly was the death of this Indian afterwards avenged. In 1794, ten years after Clarksville, Tenn., had been incorporated and named, Col. Isaac Titsworth, and his brother John, with their families, moved from North Carolina to the Cumberland country. They intended locating on Red River, and on the night of October 24, 1794, camped at the mouth of Sulphur Fork Creek, near where the Indian had been shot by Manscoe. That night a party of fifty Creek Indians stole upon them, taking them completely by surprise. Seven of the party, including Col. Titsworth and his brother, and their wives were killed and scalped. A negro woman was badly wounded, but crawled off in the woods and escaped. The Indians carried off six prisoners, a negro man, a white man, a grown daughter of Col. Titsworth, and three little children. Great excitement reigned, and in a few hours a party of white men was organized and on their trail. The Indians discovering their approach, tomahawked the children and scalped them, taking off the whole skins of their heads. The white man and the negro, they either killed or carried off with their daughter; none of the three were ever heard from."

As far back as 1807, the citizenship of Port Royal received favorable comment, as the following from "The Life and Times of Elder Reuben Ross," will show:

"Although not a great deal could be said in praise of the small village of Port Royal, in itself, near which we are now living, it would be safe to say, no finer citizenship could have been found anywhere at this time than in the country around it, extending into Robertson and Montgomery counties. In evidence of this, one need only to mention such names as Fort, Norfleet, Northington, Dortch, Baker, Cheatham, Washington, Bryant, Turner, Blount (Gov. Willie Blount), Johnson, and others. They were generally men of large stature, dignified and patriarchal in their bearing, many of them wealthy, very hospitable, and always ready to assist those who needed assistance, especially strangers who came to settle among them."

While the lordly old masters have drifted away with the "days that are dust," the posterity of a fine antebellum citizenship ligners yet with us to bless and beautify the hills and vales of dear old Port Royal.

CHAPTER XI.

"THERE IS NO DEATH, WHAT SEEMS SO, IS TRANSITION. THIS LIFE OF MORTAL BREATH, IS BUT A SUBURB OF THE LIFE ELYSIAN, WHOSE PORTAL WE CALL DEATH.

Of the four most prominent members of the Carr family, mentioned in the foregoing chapters, it is a fact worthy of note that each passed from earth from as many different States. Uncle Horace, the first to go, died near Port Royal, at his humble home on the Weatherford farm, September, 1877.

Rev. Altheus Carr died, after a short illness from fever, at Topeka, Kansas, October, 1886. He had been called to Kansas to assist in a revival, and fell, as it were, at the foot of an unfinished work. His remains were brought back to Tennessee, and laid to rest at Mount Zion, beside those of his father. The burial of no colored citizen in this section was ever so largely attended or greater demonstration of deep sorrow over the passing of a Christian leader, whose place in many respects has never been filled. His funeral orations were delivered by Revs. Houston Metcalfe, of Clarksville, Tenn., and P. Barker, of Guthrie, Ky. The latter afterward went as a missionary to Africa.

Aunt Kitty, after a short illness from pneumonia, died October, 1904, at the home of her daughter-in-law, Mrs. Margaret Manier, of Guthrie, Kentucky.

As before stated, Rev. William Carr died at Savannah, Georgia, August, 1907.

Geographically speaking, their bodies, at dissolution were widely sundered, but their kindred spirits mingled in sweet communion around the same Great White Throne.

Of a family of thirteen children, only two are living, Horace Carr, a good citizen of District No. 1, Montgomery county, Tenn., and his older sister, Mrs. Mary Waters, of Ohio.

The remainder of this chapter will be devoted to the Carneys, a family of colored citizens whose deeds should not be forgotten by those who properly appreciate the loyalty of high class antebellum negroes.

I will first speak briefly of the kind old master. Captain C. N. Carney was born in Halifax county, North Carolina, August 15th, 1782, and came to

Tennessee in 1808. He was married March 11th, 1824, to Elizabeth Johnson, of Fortson's Spring neighborhood, District No. 1, Montgomery county. There were no children by his first marriage. He was married the second time, 1848, to Miss Margaret C. Lynn, of east Montgomery county. Three sons blessed this union, viz: Richard Rodney, Thomas, and Norfleet Lynn. The first and last named still survive, and like their father, rank among the best citizens of the State. To them the writer is indebted for valuable local history gleaned by them from the early settlers of this country, with whom, by ties of blood, they were intimately associated.

The Northingtons, Johnsons Neblets, etc.

Captain Carney descended from the old Revolutionary stock, being the grandson of General Richard Rodney. The latter's sword is a cherished heirloom in the family, being owned by his namesake, R. R. Carney, of Port Royal, Tenn., who placed it for safe keeping with his brother, Dr. N. L. Carney, of Clarksville, Tenn.

Captain Carney owned a large number of valuable slaves, and a nice plantation on Parson's Creek, in District No. 5, Montgomery county. He was kind to his negroes, and they in turn were of a high order of principle, that responded to kind treatment. After a short illness from senile

Hall of Benevolent Treasure No. 7, near
Port Royal, Tennessee.

infirmities, Captain Carney died January, 1862, leaving his widow and two little boys at the old homestead, unprotected, save by these faithful family servants. Throughout the excitement incident to the Civil War, they stood true to the post of duty, as the following incident will show.

Uncle Isaac Carney, the colored blacksmith on the premises, worked for the surrounding country and people of every type came to his shop. One day a man rode up to the door on a fine young horse, that was tender footed and jaded, almost to the point of falling in its tracks. The rider dismounted and ordered it shod as quickly as possible. After it was done he drew from his purse a $20.00 greenback bill to settle. Not keeping that amount of maney at the shop in war times, the bill could not be changed, and the stranger persisted in going to the house for it. Knowing a timid woman would be frightened by the appearance of such a looking stranger, Uncle Isaac accompanied him, with his hammer in his hand. They changed the money, and on their return to the shop they were surprised to find Captain Zachary Grant, Mr. S. H. Northington, and Mr. C. Daniel waiting to arrest the guerilla horse thief, who had stolen the fine horse from a gentleman of Elkton, Ky. He was never again seen, or heard from in this section, and it was supposed they made a proper disposition of him

Uncle Isaac was born in North Carolina, February 16, 1804, and had a vivid recollection of things that took place soon after coming to Tennessee in 1808. During the war, when Southern homes were looted of valuables, Mrs. Carney entrusted her silverware and all moneys not needed by her, often as much as a thousand dollars, to Uncle Isaac, who dug a hole under his cabin floor and deposited same, which he guarded with vigilant care.

When it seemed necessary for Confederate recruiting officers to remain clandestinely in this section, for weeks at a time, Uncle Isaac often shod their horses, but in no instance was he ever known to betray one. He told of one occasion in which he felt some uneasiness. Late one evening, he was going by way of Sugar Camp branch to Bennett's distillery for a jug of whiskey when he heard threatning voices from a thick undergrowth near the roadside. A new set of recruiting officers had recently come in, and it happened to be one of these, who first saw him, and thinking he might give out information dangerous to them, they were about to sieze him, when one of the older ones, who knew him, came to his rescue, and told them to let him pass on, that he was all right.

Another of Captain Carney's valuable servants was Peter, whom he brought fom Mr. Richard Brown, of McAdoo. Peter was a Presbyterian preacher, of stout build, and ginger cake color. He was a man of very nice manners, and waited on Captain Carney, when he officiated at the musters and military parades. Aunt Sylvia was his wife. They raised a large family of children, only one of whom, Frank Carney, of Port Royal, survives.

On account of certain good qualities, Peter was allowed extra privileges over the average colored citizen of his day. He had what was termed a "general pass," permitting him to go where and when he pleased, unmolested by patrolers. He owned his own horse, and kept a shot gun. He did the neighborhood marketing, making frequent trips to Clarksville, carrying the produce on his horse, there being but few vehicles in existence. When in Clarksville, he often stopped at Hon. Cave Johnsons, a warm personal friend of his master's, or with Col. George Smith, proprietor of the old National Hotel, below where the Franklin House now stands. The last trip he ever made to Clarksville, he drove the carriage for Mrs. Carney, and Mrs. Dr. N. L. Northington.

Apropos of colored ministers, Mrs. George F. Adams, one of the best Christian women that ever blessed any community, once remarked to the writer, that she had never witnessed a more impressive antebellum picture, than that of three devout colored divines, all of different denominations, seated side by side one night at old Baker's camp meeting, listening to a soul-stirring sermon from Dr. Jno. W. Hanner, Sr. Rev. Horace Carr, Baptist; Rev. Martin Grant, Methodist, and Rev. Peter Carney, Cumberland Presbyterian. They cared little for creeds, and in their humble way preached Christ, and Him crucified.

The last record made by Captain C. N. Carney of the birth of his family servants, was that of Aleck, a valuable, bright colored man, born March 30th, 1840. When the Civil War broke out, Aleck was just twenty-one, and a man of fine appearance. In 1863, he and a fellow servant, Cæsar Carney, were pressed into service to work on a Federal fort at New Providence, Tenn. They were retained three months. While employed at work raising a steamboat sunk by the Confederates in Harpeth River, Cæsar ran away and came home, and through the influence of good friends in Clarksville, who knew Col. Bruce, the Federal officer in command, Mrs. Carney secured the release of Aleck, who gladly returned home and took up his work with Uncle Isaac in the blacksmith shop. Aleck is still in the land of the living; he owns a comfortable little home on the Port Royal road leading to Clarksville, from which, by the assistance of his son, he conducts a successful blacksmith trade, and strange to say, in his shop may be seen many of the tools he bought at the Carney sale, some of which have been in use over a century.

Among the Carney colored people, none ranked above Betsy, Aleck's sister, a fine looking yellow woman, who married Dennis Neblett, previously mentioned. No kinder heart ever beat in human breast than that of Betsy Carney-Neblett. She was a fine nurse, and would lay aside her home work any day to minister to the afflicted of her neighborhood, and when asked her charges for same, would say, "I make no charges for Christian duty."

There was an air of dignified independence in her make up, that attracted even the casual observer. For instance, she would go to church dressed in a neat plaid cotton dress, a large house-keeper's apron, and plain sailor hat, and feel as comfortable as if clad in the finest fabrics. Assisted by her economy, and thrift, her worthy husband was enabled to buy a small farm, a portion of the Carney estate, on Parson's Creek, known as the Carney Quarter.

When there was all-day meeting and dinner

on the ground at Grant's Chapel, Betsy and Dennis often went along to take charge of the dinner for some special friends, as Miss Ellen Yates, Mrs. Dr. Northington, or some of the Grants. On communion days, when Rev. J. W. Cullom was pastor in charge, he never failed to go to the church door and extend an invitation to the colored people outside to go in and partake of the Lord's Supper, and it was not uncommon to see Betsy and Dennis walk reverently down the aisle and kneel around the chancel. After a long and useful life, she passed away, ten or fifteen years ago, and her body was laid to rest on the hillside near the scene of her birth.

Henry W. Grady, the South's greatest orator and statesman, in a speech at Boston, Mass., a few years before his death, gave a battlefield experience that was eloquently pathetic. He said:

"In sad memory I see a young Confederate soldier struck by a fatal bullet, stagger and fall, and I see a black and shambling figure make his way through a throng of soldiers, wind his loving arms about him, and bear him from the field of carnage, and from the pale lips of that dying friend, I hear a feeble voice bidding me to follow that black hero and protect him, if he ever needed protection, and I was true to my promise."

We who love Southern soil, and cherish Southern

tradition, should pause now and then and pay due tribute not only to the worthy living, but to the faithful colored dead "who sleep out under the stars!"

CPSIA information can be obtained
at www.ICGtesting.com
Printed in the USA
BVOW06s2005030217

475148BV00012BB/206/P